The Usborne Book of
Everyday Words
in English

Designer and modelmaker: Jo Litchfield

Editors: Rebecca Treays, Kate Needham and Lisa Miles
Photography: Howard Allman
Additional models by: Stefan Barnett
Managing Editor: Felicity Brooks
Managing Designer: Mary Cartwright
Photographic manipulation and design: Michael Wheatley

With thanks to Inscribe Ltd. and Eberhard Faber for providing the Fimo® modelling material

Everyday Words is a stimulating and lively wordfinder for young children. Each double page shows familiar scenes from the world around us, providing plenty of opportunity for talking and sharing.

Very young children will have fun simply spotting and naming the different objects and characters. Children who are beginning to learn to read will enjoy reading the words around the edges of the scenes. This book will also be a useful spelling guide for older children who are starting to write their own stories.

A word list at the back of the book brings together all the words in alphabetical order. This can be used to encourage children to look up words and find the right page and picture – an important skill which will prepare them for the later use of dictionaries and information books.

There are a number of hidden objects to find in every big scene. A small picture shows what to look for.

Above all, this bright and busy book will give children hours of enjoyment and a love of reading that will last.

The family

sister   brother   daughter   father   son   mother

cat   grandmother   grandfather   dog

 grandson    granddaughter

The town

 Find fifteen cars

petrol station

supermarket

shops

hospital

swimming pool

school

car park

cinema

bridge

The street

Find twelve birds

baker's

waiter

police officer

chemist

pushchair

bus stop

6

butcher's

dog

café

skateboard

firefighter

pram

lamppost

post office

cat

baker

The house

Find eight cups

door   door handle   carpet   roof   bannister

attic

bedroom   study   bathroom

living room   hall   kitchen

fireplace   light switch   rug   window   stairs

q

The garden

caterpillar

flowerpot

bee

hoe

bone

slug

ladybird

leaf

snail

ant

rake

kennel

tree

barbecue

butterfly

wheelbarrow

seeds

nest

lawnmower

The kitchen

sink

knife

Find ten tomatoes

washing machine

toaster

chair

saucer

table

cup

frying pan

microwave

fork

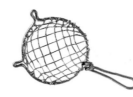

sieve

cooker

spoon

dustpan

dishwasher

plate

saucepan

jug

bowl

fridge

13

Things to eat

biscuit

bread

pasta

rice

flour

cereal

fruit juice

tea bag

coffee

sugar

milk

cream

butter

egg

cheese

yoghurt

chicken

prawn

sausage

bacon

fish

salami

ham

soup

pizza

salt

pepper

mustard

ketchup

honey

jam

raisins

peanuts

water

pineapple

pear

lime

lemon

peach

apricot

cherry

banana

strawberry

raspberry

mango

grapefruit

plum

coconut

orange

watermelon

melon

grapes

apple

kiwi fruit

tomato

avocado

potato

green beans

courgette

cabbage

onion

mushroom

carrot

aubergine

leek

broccoli

cauliflower

peas

spinach

beetroot

lettuce

celery

sweetcorn

cucumber

chilli

pepper

15

The living room

CD

Find four mugs

purse

armchair

vacuum cleaner

DVD

sofa

DVD player

stereo

jigsaw

television

recorder

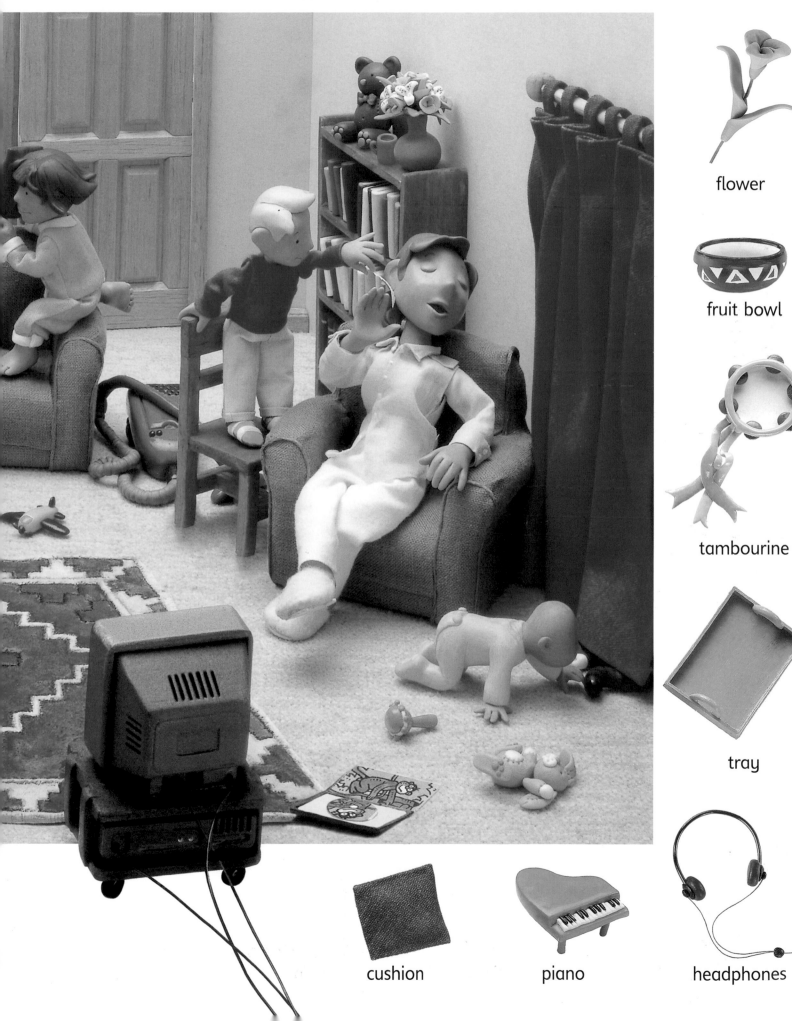

flower

fruit bowl

tambourine

tray

cushion

piano

headphones

The study

Find nine pens

desk

computer

telephone

magazine

guitar

plant

book

crayon

photograph

18

The bathroom

 Find three boats

soap

basin

towel

plug

toilet

bath

toilet paper

comb

shampoo

shower

The bedroom

 Find four spiders

 crocodile

 trumpet

 chest of drawers

robot

 bed

 teddy bear

rocket

 doll

drum

spaceship

elephant

radio

snake

alarm clock

puppet

bedside table

lion

blanket

giraffe

playing cards

21

Around the house

toothpaste

toothbrush

newspaper

letter

blind

curtain

duvet

pillow

photograph
album

ironing board

iron

sewing machine

vase

computer mouse

potty

sponge

tap

hairbrush

mirror

bin

washing-up liquid

calculator

toys

lamp

Transport

ambulance

fire engine

police car

helicopter

lorry

car

digger

scooter

boat

canoe

caravan

plane

hot-air balloon

tractor

taxi

bicycle

bus

motorbike

submarine

train

racing car

van

cable car

sports car

The farm

 Find five kittens

piglet

pig

goose

bull

cow

calf

cockerel

chick

hen

24

barn

rabbit

sheep

lamb

pond

donkey

goat

farmer

turkey

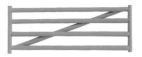

gate

duckling

duck

puppy

horse

The classroom

 Find twenty crayons

pencil sharpener

easel

pen

paper

felt-tip pen

chalk

coat hook

scissors

chalkboard

26

string

stool

pencil

rubber

tape

glue

blocks

paint

paintbrush

clock

exercise book

ruler

teacher

The party

Find eleven apples

CD player

present

pirate

cowboy

doctor

crisps

popcorn

balloon

ribbon

28

cake

chocolate

ice cream

card

ballerina

mermaid

astronaut

clown

sweet

candle

straw

highchair

29

The campsite

 Find two teddies

tent

camera

radio

rucksack

torch

passport

money

football

umbrella

map

binoculars

kitten

ticket

Things to wear

T-shirt

jeans

dungarees

dress

skirt

tights

pyjamas

dressing gown

vest

bib

jumper

sweatshirt

cardigan

trousers

apron

shirt

coat

tracksuit

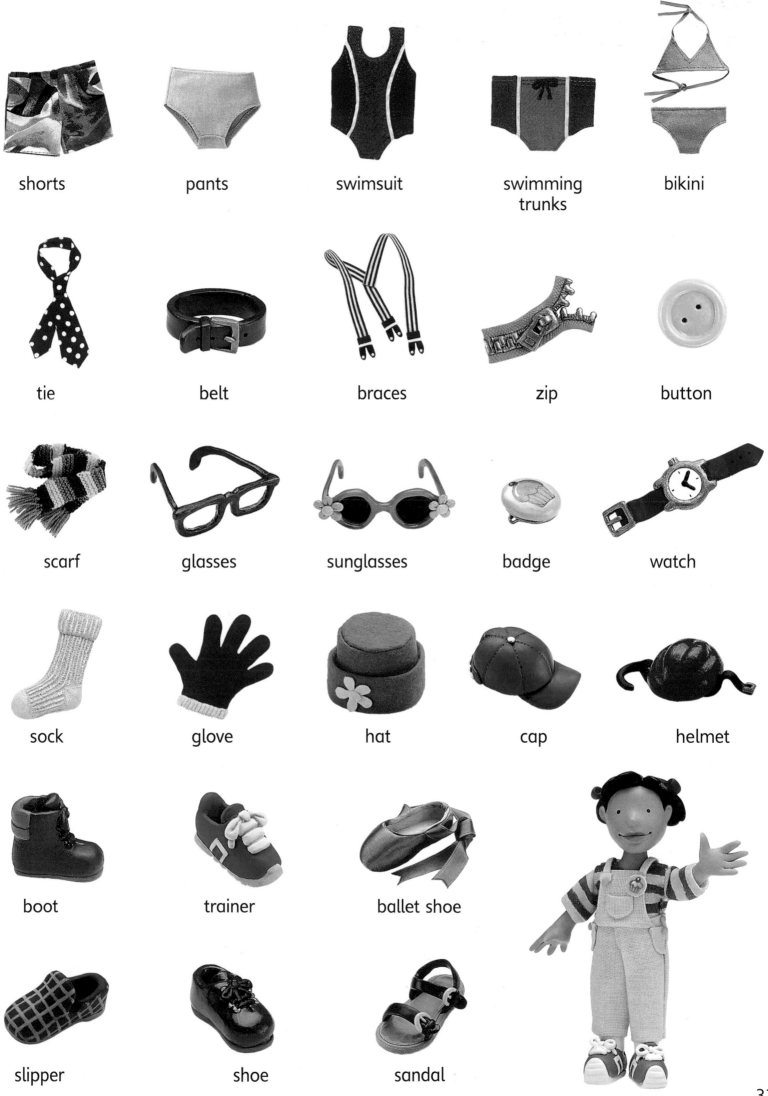

shorts

pants

swimsuit

swimming trunks

bikini

tie

belt

braces

zip

button

scarf

glasses

sunglasses

badge

watch

sock

glove

hat

cap

helmet

boot

trainer

ballet shoe

slipper

shoe

sandal

The workshop

 Find thirteen mice

toolbox

watering can

nail

hammer

penknife

screwdriver

tin

spider

34

 saw

 vice

 key

 worm

 bucket

 spade

 match

 cardboard box

 wheel

 hose

 rope

moth

spanner

 broom

35

The park

 Find seven footballs

boy

36

 bird

 sandwich

 tennis racket

 hamburger

 kite

 baby

 hotdog

 chips

 wheelchair

 girl

swings

seesaw

roundabout

 slide

37

Parts of the body

head

ear

tongue

nose

mouth

teeth

eye

back

tummy

tummy button

arm

leg

elbow

knee

hand

foot

finger

thumb

bottom

long hair

short hair

curly hair

straight hair

Actions

sleeping

cycling

riding

smiling

laughing

crying

singing

walking

running

jumping

kicking

writing   painting   drawing   reading   cutting   sticking

sitting   standing   pushing   pulling

eating   drinking   bathing   kissing   waving

Shapes

oval

circle

crescent

triangle

square

rectangle

star

Colours

red

pink

yellow

brown

grey

blue

purple

white

green

black

orange

42

Numbers

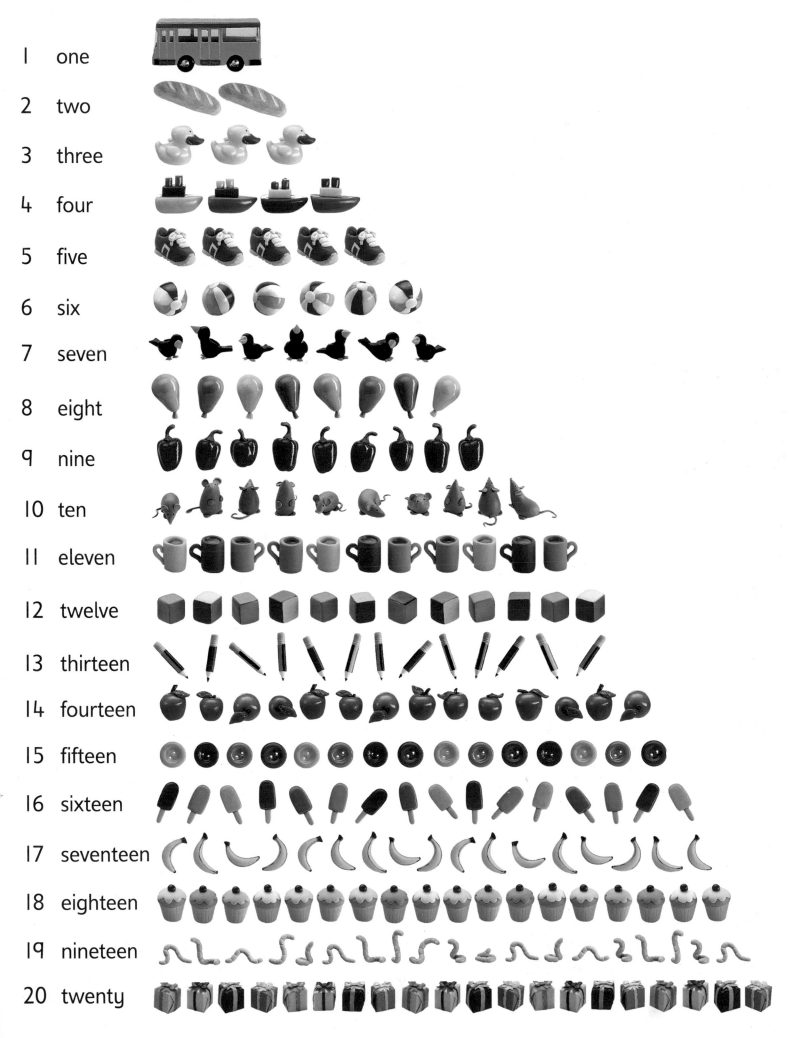

1 one

2 two

3 three

4 four

5 five

6 six

7 seven

8 eight

9 nine

10 ten

11 eleven

12 twelve

13 thirteen

14 fourteen

15 fifteen

16 sixteen

17 seventeen

18 eighteen

19 nineteen

20 twenty

Word list

a actions, 40-41
alarm clock, 21
ambulance, 23
ant, 11
apple, 15
apples, 28
apricot, 15
apron, 32
arm, 39
armchair, 16
astronaut, 29
attic, 9
aubergine, 15
avocado, 15

b baby, 37
back (part of
  body), 38
bacon, 14
badge, 33
baker, 7
baker's, 6
ballerina, 29
ballet shoe, 33
balloon, 28
banana, 15
bannister, 8
barbecue, 11
barn, 25
basin, 19
bath, 19
bathroom, 9, 19
bed, 20
bedroom, 9, 20-21
bedside table, 21
bee, 10
beetroot, 15
belt, 33
bib, 32
bicycle, 23

bikini, 33
bin, 22
binoculars, 31
bird, 37
birds, 6
biscuit, 14
black, 42
blanket, 21
blind, 22
blocks, 27
blue, 42
boat, 23
boats, 19
body, 38-39
bone, 10
book, 18
boot, 33
bottom (part of
  body), 39
bowl, 13
boy, 36
braces, 33
bread, 14
bridge, 5
broccoli, 15
broom, 35
brother, 3
brown, 42
bucket, 35
bull, 24
bus, 23
bus stop, 6
butcher's, 7
butter, 14
butterfly, 11
button, 33

c cabbage, 15
cable car, 23
café, 7

cake, 29
calculator, 22
calf, 24
camera, 30
campsite, 30-31
candle, 29
canoe, 23
cap, 33
car, 23
cars, 4
car park, 5
caravan, 23
card, 29
cardboard box, 35
cardigan, 32
carpet, 8
carrot, 15
cat, 7
caterpillar, 10
cauliflower, 15
CD, 16
CD player, 28
celery, 15
cereal, 14
chair, 12
chalk, 26
chalkboard, 26
cheese, 14
chemist, 6
cherry, 15
chest of drawers, 20
chick, 24
chicken, 14
chilli, 15
chips, 37
chocolate, 29
cinema, 5
circle, 42
classroom, 26-27
clock, 27

Additional models: Les Pickstock, Barry Jones, Stef Lumley and Karen Krige.
With thanks to Vicki Groombridge, Nicole Irving and the
Model Shop, 151 City Road, London.